Options Trading

Simplified Options Trading Guide for Generating Profits on an Ongoing Basis

By Erik Vinny

© Copyright 2014 by Erik Vinny- All rights reserved.

This document is geared towards providing exact and reliable information in regards to the topic and issue covered. The publication is sold with the idea that the publisher is not required to render accounting, officially permitted, or otherwise, qualified services. If advice is necessary, legal or professional, a practiced individual in the profession should be ordered.

- From a Declaration of Principles which was accepted and approved equally by a Committee of the American Bar Association and a Committee of Publishers and Associations.

In no way is it legal to reproduce, duplicate, or transmit any part of this document in either electronic means or in printed format. Recording of this publication is strictly prohibited and any storage of this document is not allowed unless with written permission from the publisher. All rights reserved.

The information provided herein is stated to be truthful and consistent, in that any liability, in terms of inattention or otherwise, by any usage or abuse of any policies, processes, or directions contained within is the solitary and utter responsibility of the recipient reader. Under no circumstances will any legal responsibility or blame be held against the publisher for any reparation, damages, or monetary loss due to the information herein, either directly or indirectly.

Respective authors own all copyrights not held by the publisher.

The information herein is offered for informational purposes solely, and is universal as so. The presentation of the information is without contract or any type of guarantee assurance.

The trademarks that are used are without any consent, and the publication of the trademark is without permission or backing by the trademark owner. All trademarks and brands within this book are for clarifying purposes only and are the owned by the owners themselves, not affiliated with this document.

Table of Contents

Introduction 1

Chapter 1: Why Choose Options? 2

Chapter 2: Simple Guidelines that will Make you an Expert Trader 11

Chapter 3: Why a Margin Account is Necessary for All Strategies 18

Chapter 4: Basic Trading Strategies 20

Chapter 5: The Importance of an Exit Strategy 27

Chapter 6: Fundamental Analysis Information 29

Chapter 7: The "Common Sense" Strategy for Trading Options 29

Conclusion 43

Introduction

I want to thank you and congratulate you for downloading the book, *"Options Trading: Simplified Options Trading Guide for Generating Profits on an Ongoing Basis"*.

This book contains proven steps and strategies on how to learn all you need to know about constructing an options trading strategy.

When someone makes a decision to do their own research about options trading, they will not run into a lack of information. So, how is one to find out how to separate the valuable information from the nonsense? The key is to expose yourself to as much differing information as possible, and then begin constructing your strategies from there. .

Thanks again for downloading this book, I certainly hope you enjoy it!

Chapter 1: Why Choose Options Trading?

There are a lot of different choices out there as to which trading to partake in. So, why do people choose options? The number one reason for choosing options is that you can invest smaller amounts of capital while controlling bigger amounts of different stock, especially when it comes to call options. These options cost less than their underlying asset, always, and put options are typically also cheaper.

The Volatility of Options Means Higher Action:

In general, options tend to be volatile more than the underlying assets. This means that people who invest in them are typically getting more action with the stock. Obviously, this can lead to risky situations, but you will learn that it can also mean more security and safety with your money. You will also learn that you can enjoy more flexibility with your trades and also earn profits when you aren't sure about which way the stock will go. To summarize, options trading allow investors to enjoy flexibility, higher risk protection, and the potential to gain more for any specific motion in the price of the stock. On the other hand, this can lead to serious issues and losses if used wrongly.

Why are Options Known, Comparatively, as such Risky Endeavors?

You may have heard, especially while becoming interested in general trading, that options is a risky way to trade. Why are options given this label and constantly referred to as risky and dangerous compared to other types of trading? What is the best way to understand this and view options as a way to limit dangers and risk to our capital? It is perfectly possible to maximize your potential for high returns and learn from what you are doing, as you do it. That is the essence of what this guide is all about; making confusing and complex material into information that is easy and simple to digest for anyone who commits to learning about it.

Options trading has turned into a highly popular method for trading, particularly in the United States. Rather than being confined to financial experts or prestigious institutions, this method of trading is seen as quite mainstream for traders from everywhere. The whole idea of trading options is still looked at with trepidation and fear by many, however. When people first embark upon this path, they will receive warnings from concerned friends more often than not. But, it turns out that options trading is only as dangerous as you decide to make it. This brings me to the next important point.

Successful Trading is all about the Right Strategy:

An inescapable fact that you must accept now, is that there are no short cuts, and only constructing a personal plan for trading will get you anywhere in this world. This means that you are ensuring that your risks are as low as possible and that your potentials are as high as possible. You must have a plan that is structured in a simple way that you understand fully, ensuring that you know how to follow its rules each time you trade. Many professional traders simplify their plans as they progress in trading, rather than gaining more and more complex methods as they go, as one might assume.

How to Become a Successful Investor in Options Trading:

To become a successful options trader, you have to work on these traits. Luckily, if you weren't born with them, they can be learned and improved over time. Of course, the more you practice each of these, the better they will become.

- **Honesty with Yourself:** Trading can get difficult when you do it alone instead of with professional guidance. This means that you are relying on your own wits and will power. To effectively do this, you have to learn how to be honest with yourself in a realistic way. Do you trust your own judgment and voice? If not, you need to work on this before getting started on your options trading career.

  If you have hopes of becoming a successful or even decent investor or trader, you must learn the art of self-honesty. When it comes down to it, the results you experience are what decide how talented you will be in this realm. The decisions you make are up to you and you only. Deciding to blame things on other people will not help you whatsoever. Once you commit to a course of action, it's all about where you decide to go with it.

- **Planning Ahead:** If planning was never your strong suit, it's time to change that. Deciding to "go with the flow" may be a great philosophy in some areas of life, but when it comes to options trading, having a plan is a better course of action. This will keep you safe from whims or temptations of the moment, which will always crop up, no matter what. If you aren't prepared for this, you will inevitably fall victim to it.

- **Developing Self-Discipline:** How good are you at controlling your own impulses? If you don't know the answer to this question, trading will give you insight into that area very quickly. However, this is something you should master ideally before getting involved, otherwise the lesson could come at a high financial cost. Developing self-discipline ahead of time means that you are not risking getting overwhelmed and fed up with the options trading world before you even give it a fair shot.

- **Commitment to Persevere:** Rome was not built in a day, as the saying goes. This means that if you hope to enjoy vast success with options trading, you have to be willing to put in the work. Get this through your head right away, if you haven't already; there are no shortcuts here. If you have it in your mind that you will be the next big overnight millionaire from trading options, you should step back and re-evaluate before you take another step. People who have hopes like this will view options trading as gambling rather than a method that requires respect, and that is simply the wrong approach to have.

When you want to give up, keep on going. If you truly have belief in a certain thing, you must stay with it until you accomplish your deepest goals. As soon as you have reached your target, set to work coming up with another goal. Since you have taken on the aspiration to get great at trading (either on the side or as a fulltime pursuit), you have to stay with it if you have any chance to make it. Don't make the mistake of assuming that some are capable of following this path and others aren't, because it simply isn't true. Anyone can do this who commits to it.

It's happened many times before. The most unlikely people become great at trading when they start out thinking it's not possible for them. In order to stay practical about it, allow yourself targets that are attainable and can be achieve within a time frame that is realistic given your circumstances. For example, you can decide that in one week you will have a full understanding of the main risk categories for options profiles. You may even be able to reach this goal sooner than you plan initially.

Make it a point to set goals that are attainable, but still challenging, and this will let you get the momentum going for learning as you go and getting plenty of experience. You will also begin building up your self-confidence as you get better, allowing yourself to see that you can gain understanding of any subject you decide to learn about. This guide is a great place to start in your journey because it is full of valuable information but also simple to follow. So continue on and enjoy your learning process.

- **Gaining the Right Knowledge:** As mentioned in the introduction to this book, there is no shortage of trading information out there, especially since the internet is so popular and widely available in modern day. So, how do you find out what information is quality? It's simple. Apply the information you find and see if it works for you. There is something that is very important to remember with trading, and I will say it a few different times in this book and in a few different ways; there is no one size fits all method with options.

    This is a highly personal journey that only you can pick the perfect strategy for. Other people can provide you with valuable insight and tools, but it's up to you to piece it together, with your own personal elements added in, in a way that suits you perfectly.

A Patient Attitude Must be Adopted in Trading Options:

Earning a lot of capital on the market is among the most thrilling of experiences someone can have in terms of earning an income. There are two main ways that this can be done. The first involves earning thousands of gains in percentage every time you trade (which has more to do with luck than skill). The second is taking time to develop and hone the skills necessary to succeed. There is no rush here. Make the effort to take your time building up strategies that will be useful to you time and time again, and take the time to perfect your skills as a trader.

There will, if you stick with this path, eventually come a day when you feel confident and certain about your knowledge about the market, but how can you tell if this is a genuine sentiment or just wishful and impatient thinking? When you can look at a variety of opportunities and only make a trade when you see the most obvious choice, turning down opportunities that are substandard without getting too upset about it, you will know you have reached the point of being ready.

Why would you Rush this Process?

When you are new to trading, there is no reason or excuse to rush the process. Consider it like this, would you feel that you were prepared to perform surgery on someone after reading only one guide on the subject? It is highly unlikely that you would. Well, thinking of trading in the same way. Allow yourself plenty of time to learn the necessary information, and don't expect miracles. By reading this guide, you're already on the right path and already giving a valuable learning opportunity to yourself. If you know how stocks function already, this here is what you should do next. Similar to the way you had to take time to get familiar with stock trading, you have to view options trading in the same way.

Patience is Necessary for More than just Learning about Trading Options:

But patience is not just needed for the learning process. Once you do reach a level of familiarity that allows you to feel comfortable trading, you have to be patient enough to actually follow through on it. Think of it as not only an educational process for earning money, but also for improving your personality by becoming more patient and humble. Everyone has had an experience where they jumped too early into an investment, although they had their doubts in the back of their mind. This will not pay off in the long run. Instead, remember to have patience, breathe deeply when necessary, and stay with the plan you took so much time and effort to construct.

Patience is a Key Component in your Successful Trading Strategy:

In addition, being patient has a lot to do with choosing a strategy for trading that allows time to work in your best interest and where you also have the downside well covered. Countless strategies exist out there for you to pick from, but wise investors always choose to keep it simple, understanding that complicating matters does not always pay off in the end. No matter which strategy you decide to go with, always commit to waiting until the best opportunity shows up. You can choose your favorite patterns on the charts and wait until they appear before you decide to trade. When a person specializes, they earn the most, so make it your goal to become a trading specialist.

Apathy vs. Patience in Trading:

When it comes to gaining wealth, you should always have a patient approach and attitude. The more you can attain this approach, the more potential you will have as an options trader. Make no mistake, this has nothing to do with sitting idle and waiting around for opportunities to happen to you. That is what separates apathy from being truly patient. Allow time for yourself to learn the process, get the experience you need, and begin applying the principles you learn in a consistent way that allows you to build capital and earn money regularly.

Learn the Art of Compounding Small Percentage Returns:

An important aspect of patience in trading is learning how to compound. Think of it this way, if you earn only a single percent every week, this will add up to over 52 percent in only a single year, which is a decent overall return. Instead of viewing this as a process where you aim to make large amounts at a single time, let your returns build up over time, allowing the compounding to do most of the earning work. In the moment, it doesn't seem like you're earning much, but learn to see the big picture.

This is what separates the professional and expert traders who enjoy profits in the long term from people who jump into trading and jump out just as quickly. The experts treat this process with respect and know about the art of compounding. If you hope to make a successful career out of trading, you will learn this art as well.

Chapter 2: Simple Guidelines that will Make you an Expert Trader

A lot of people have a misconception about trading being a complex subject reserved only for number geniuses or retired folks, but this is simply not the case. In fact, there are some very easily understandable and simple guidelines that any beginner trader can follow to enjoy success in the world of options trading. Here are the basics.

Take Full Advantage of the Freedom of Information Era:

Since we've already gone over how necessary becoming patient is in both the learning process and in the actual process of trading, we should keep in mind that information is so available that nearly anyone can learn to trade in a reasonable amount of time. There are tools out there right now that effectively simulate the experience of trading with no risk at all. There are also countless websites and publications that are specially designed to help you build up your database of trading knowledge. Although theoretical knowledge will help you a lot, it's true that experience is the best teacher out there, so be smart and combine both of these to become highly effective in options trading.

Work with, not against your Emotions:

A lot of trading guides will advise you against letting your emotions take you over and make decisions for you during a trade. And while it makes sense in theory to tell people that they should trade free of emotion, rarely anyone actually achives this. Feelings are a part of being human, and there's no escaping that. So, instead of trying to ignore this fact, you should work to learn how to use them constructively in your strategies. This is what many successful traders do; stay in the safe zone but still allow themselves to play for larger returns. Having the correct mindset is more important than nearly anything else here.

Use Extremes to your Learning Advantage:

Keep in mind at all times, that any type of learning comes from direct experience. Everyone can easily remember extreme people they have met from the past. They can remember their scariest teacher from school, the meanest, or the nicest. However, as easy as it is to remember these figures, how easy is it to remember the ones that fell somewhere near the middle on the scale? It is significantly more difficult to remember the ones who made little impact, and the same principle is at work with trading.

Experience is the Best Teacher in Both Life and Options:

Most of the learning you will undertake with options trading is based purely on your own experience. As a matter of fact, the most effective of all learning when it comes to options trading has to do with direct experience. Extreme and memorable experiences are the ones that will teach you the most about not only trading, but the way your own mind and impulses work. The best traders out there have had extremely bad experiences with trading, but have been able to get back up and use the experience to make them better.

A lot of beginners fall into a trap of thinking that since they were able to earn cash fast at the beginning, they are invincible. If you do this, you will quickly discover that that is not the case. Although it won't feel great for traders, at the time, to learn these lessons, they are useful. So, let yourself gain knowledge from the tough experiences and remember to stick with simplicity.

Knowing how to Plan Effectively in Trading Options:

Each and every time you embark on a trade, you have to plan ahead. A trader is only as good as the plans he trades with. What this entails is a constant commitment to the following:

- **Minimizing Risks:** Thinking ahead to make sure that you are avoiding danger as much as possible. Obviously, no matter what you're trading, there is some measure of risk involved, since that is how trading is at its core, but it is perfectly possible to minimize this a lot, and all professional traders know exactly how to do so.

- **Maximizing Rewards:** Since the entire point of trading is to try to earn money, this might be an obvious one, but it still pays (literally) to keep this principle in mind at all times. You will run into trades where minimizing risk is more important than maximizing rewards, vice versa, and also mixes of the two.

- **Figuring out Pre-planned Points of Entry:** Every trader needs to have standards, or minimum requirements for what a trade looks like before they will enter it or even give it a second thought. Decide ahead of time, before you get tempted into rationalizing subpar conditions, what your standards are, and stick to them. This way you will avoid entering trades that are dead ends.

- **Figuring out Pre-planned Exit Strategies:** Where most traders fail is beginning to win and getting too greedy, throwing out everything they have earned because they hope to go even higher. This is why deciding on a "break even point" is a must in trading options. You decide how much you want to earn and exit the trade once you reach that point. Without deciding this ahead of time, you run the risk of going too far and losing.

When it comes to trading options, you should base your stop losses on what the underlying stock's basis is. It is a fact of trading options that the underlying stock is a lot more liquid than the options that come along with it. This means that it's much easier to make decisions for cutting losses considering the stock's price, underlying asset, or the future of that stock. The most important and primary part of planning ahead is how you choose the underlying stock based on the pattern of its chart. Then you can be on your way to making a plan for trading.

Discipline, What all Successful Traders Know about:

With options trading, discipline can be considered the cornerstone of being successful. Once you have acquired enough patience to gain the necessary knowledge and go through the processes discussed earlier, you must be sure not to waste what you've learned. You have to be disciplined enough to apply the principles every time they are relevant. If you stay disciplined, you will:

- **Plan Ahead with Each and Every Trade.**
- **Use the Experience of Yourself and Others.**
- **Stick with your Plan no Matter What.**

In doing all of this, you will be on the path to becoming a methodical and successful trader. Acquiring discipline is not an optional part of trading successfully. Without knowing how to manage your money, systems of trading won't work, no matter how complex or sophisticated they are. By standing by your principles for managing money no matter what, you will make sure that you minimize your losses and allow your profits to run freely and to their highest potential.

Avoiding Dangerous Profiles for Risk Management:

Committing to a disciplined approach will also cover an important aspect of options trading; avoiding dangerous profiles for risk. A lot of experts teach strategies for options that have incredibly dangerous curves on their risk profiles. While the temptation of earning big and quickly can often cause traders to throw caution to the win, this is more akin to gambling than actual trading and is not recommended.

Why you should Use Time Frames in your Trading:

Every successful trader should know about time frames. These are a valuable tool that was created with the intention of giving you access to the secrets of the market in multiple ways. The complication with showing the movements of the market is the sheer number of these movements. Popular assets are especially prone to moving every which way very quickly, creating an overabundance of information about it.

One of the best ways to stay on top of time frames is by using candlesticks, which was developed by traders who specialize in technical analysis. They display the movements of prices on charts, allowing you to look closely at movements without missing any action. You can rest assured that you are receiving all of the information you need, in an easy-to-digest manner that will aid you in making an informed choice with your trade. For this reason, all traders should educate themselves about general time frames as well as the specific candlestick method.

Signal Providers for Options Trading:

A signal in options is defined as an alert given by text, audio, or e-mail giving advice to the trader as to the most promising trading options. These signals are created by the analyzing of the trends and charts about the price movement of an asset. Then, a movement is predicted and sent to benefit the trader. There are a few different signal providers out there, and here are the best.

Quantum Binary Signals: This provider offers a service that is simple and easy, allowing traders to have access to options without doing any of their own analyzing. The provider gives detailed and thorough steps to follow to enjoy success with their signals and allows traders to enjoy quality returns. Whether you are a beginner or professional trader, the strategies provided by Quantum will help you along the way with accumulating better returns.

Option Robot: This provider uses a complicated process for creating its signals, meaning that they are very accurate and high quality. In fact, the signals of Option Robot have one of the best ranking win rates in the entire industry, coming out at over 80%!

Binary Hedge Fund: This service is one of the best and most advanced out there and also gives some of the best signals while staying secure and safe. The signals provided by Binary Hedge are given with plenty of analysis and putting together of both past and current data, spanning back multiple years in the options market. This software is free, simple to use, and has a quality ratio for winning.

Chapter 3: Why a Margin Account is Necessary for All Strategies

One of the first things an investor should think about, especially when starting out in trading options, is creating a margin account. The requirement for this margin is how much money and securities are necessary with a deposit to fully take care of the risks of a broker. The mechanism of a margin account will make sure that you have the right amount of collateral for any activity in trading. This is particularly necessary for traders who enjoy short selling, naked selling, or trading spreads with net credit.

The Difference between Margin for Stock Trading and Options Trading:

For trading stock, having this margin will work as a mechanism for providing leverage, or money that has been borrowed, to increase the amount of one's holdings. When it comes to options, this is not the case, since the margin is solely used to ensure that there is enough collateral involved. When someone purchases an amount of shares, they typically either use their margin account (in essence, borrowing the money from a brokerage), or for this or pay in cash for up to half of the percentage of the price for the share purchase.

The margin for maintenance is decided upon ahead of time to make sure that the margin account's balance doesn't ever go into the negative. There have been times that this was set to about a quarter of the percentage of the shares' value, but it can vary widely. When someone purchases either put or call options, they have to pay the price for purchase fully. It is not possible to purchase options using margin since the options already have a significant amount of leverage within them, and using margin to purchase options would bring the leverage levels up to unacceptable heights. In this case, margin relates to the requirements for collateral.

A Margin Account as Protective Measure in Options Trading:

The naked writing (or selling) of options means that no trades for covering exist for hedging the naked sale's risk. This means that, when selling naked put or call options, you should keep money in the margin account to use for collateral. This will make sure that the writer of the options doesn't choose to default their obligation if the buyer of the options uses or exercises their right. The amount of this margin will vary according to which type of trade has been entered.

When someone is selling short or is trading a spread involved with net credit, there will be funds deposited into their account because of the trade, but a risk for contingent liability still exists, which has to be covered by your account's funds. This money can either exist as securities that are marginable or actual cash. A security that is considered marginable is some type of asset that has been deemed secure enough by a brokerage to act as the collateral that will stand on the trade up against the risk. AAPL, or other stocks that are considered blue chip, could be called marginable securities. Stocks that are priced low (less than 10 dollars), however, that do not have much history with trading, don't have high volume for trading, and have a lot of volatility, cannot work as collateral in this case.

Chapter 4: Basic Trading Strategies

The best and most effective strategies for trading are highly personalized. Since only you are fully aware of what your personality, financial situation, and abilities are, only you can decide the right path for you. In this chapter, I will give you some basic strategy components that you can use to construct your very own trading method. Remember that trading strategies are meant to be tested, altered, and perfected. Eventually, you will come to a strategy that seems to work the majority of the time, but it's always possible to improve and get even better with time.

That being said, every quality trading strategy involves the basics. As you advance in your knowledge of options trading and decide you are ready to construct your own strategy, there are some key terms you will need to familiarize yourself with:

Different Options Types- Puts and Calls:

- **Puts:** A put refers to having the option (choice) to sell. This type of option gives you the right to sell off a particular asset at a determined price before the date of expiration, without obligating you to do so.

- **Calls:** A call refers to having the option (choice) to purchase. This type of option gives one the right to purchase an asset at a certain price before its expiration date, without obligating them to do so.

Now that we have gone over the basic definitions of calls and puts, which is necessary information for traders at every level, we can review the different types.

Different Types of Put and Call Options:

- **American Style Options:** These types of options let the buyer of the option exercise their right with the option on any date, as long as it is before the date of expiration. The majority of traded options are actually American style, and every option that is U.S. equity is, as well. These are a bit more valuable than their European counterparts, since they offer more flexibility. It stands to reason that the ability to exercise an option before it expires is a more valuable option than not having that choice.

- **European Style Options:** These types of options do not let the buyer of the option exercise their right with the option before the date of expiration.

Typically, options that are involved in stock are of the American style variety, while options that are involved in futures are European. To put it simply and in laymen's terms, options are when you have a right to sell or purchase an asset at a specific and decided price before or on a specific date. It also means that you are not obligated to do so. There are some key components to pay attention to in this definition:

- **A Right, but not an Obligation.**
- **Selling or Purchasing an Asset.**
- **A Decided Price.**

- **Before or on a Specific Date.**

These key components all have very important implications on how valuable an option actually is. Keep in mind that an option has value itself, as well, but before we get into the different ways that the value of options are decided, let's go over what it means to have a right without an obligation.

A Right, but not an Obligation:

People buy options because they then receive the right to call (purchase) or put (sell) the asset that is underlying (this could be a share, for example). When you make a purchase on an option, this does not obligate you to sell or buy the underlying asset. You only, technically, are able to do this at the price that is fixed (also known as the strike or exercise price). The risk you are accepting when you purchase an option is only the amount you used to pay for it.

Selling Options Naked and What that Determines:

When you sell naked, you have an obligation imposed. You are now obliged to purchase from (using puts that have been sold) or deliver (using calls that have been sold) to the buyer of the options if they decide to exercise their right. Opting for the naked selling of options (such as when you haven't purchased an underlying asset position or options to hedge with it) means that you will have a profile with unlimited risk involved in it.

This is Generally Advised Against for Beginners:

Considering the fact that you are also obligated to take action, it is generally recommended that you shouldn't take this type of position, especially when you are new to the game of options trading. Only the most expert and advanced of traders should consider the naked selling of options. Even if they do, they should always have a strategy decided upon ahead of time that can protect against potential downside dangers.

Deciding to Actually Place the Trade:

For most of you reading this, it's safe to assume that you will be placing your trades on the internet. Since the prices for options are not considered "clean", always, it is much preferred to use a limit order, especially when it comes to spreads. This will make sure that your orders get filled using the price you specified, or they don't get filled at all.

Different Types of Orders to Know About:

In order to construct your perfect strategy, there are a number of terms to know about. Here is a general list to help you with that:

- **Limit Orders:** When it comes to limit orders, you will be either buying when a share goes down to a specific price or falls lower than that, or selling when a share rises up to a specific price or higher than that. With options, limits are generally recommended, especially with combination trades and spreads. This is because the spread prices for bid-ask can change drastically, which doesn't always happen to your benefit, meaning that it's preferable to be specific about your pricing.

- **Market Orders:** When it comes to these types of orders, you will be authorizing a broker to sell or purchase options or stock using their judgment to find the best quality of price available on the market at the time.

- **Buy Stop Orders:** These refer to the times that you purchase only once a stock has gotten to or gone beyond a specified price. Contrary to the limit order when you purchase the stock after it has fallen, buy stops fit in when you expect the stock to go up past a level of resistance or go up from a basic support level.

- **Sell Stop or Stop Loss:** This refers to when you decide to sell if a stock goes under a specific price. A sell stop is always put under the price at the current time and you can always increase your stop loss if it turns out that the share goes up.

Trade Orders that come with Time Limits:

If you aren't aware of the time limits that come along with some options, you may end up in a sticky situation or two. In order to better prepare you for encountering these, I will give a basic list of which orders to watch for and pay attention to.

- **Fill or Kill Orders:** These orders are considered the highest priority of all, since they are canceled unless they are fulfilled right away. An order that is fill or kill will inevitably grab a floor trader's attention. However, if this is also a limit order, it has to be as realistic as possible as well.

- **GTC (or good 'till cancelled):** This refers to the situation where an order stays valid until or unless you either fill it or cancel it altogether. To put it another way, a GTC limit order refers to you having authorized a broker to purchase stock at a specified amount or lower than that amount, either today or another, later date when it is selling at the specified amount of money, up until you've purchased an amount of shares that is requisite. You should always exercise caution with these types of orders since they usually don't hit the tops of floor traders' priority lists.

- **All or None Orders:** This is quite self-explanatory and means that the entire order either has to be filled at the same time, or none of it will be. Typically, these are not a smart choice since a lot of trades are not filled in full anyway, since there must be either a seller or buyer on the opposite side, and usually they will not be dealing specifically with the same sizes of lots that your order is. This means that you should not go for all or none if you have hopes of getting the order filled.

- **Week Only Orders:** This refers to orders that are cancelled if they are not fulfilled by the end of the week.

- **Day Only Order:** This refers to an order that will get cancelled if it hasn't been fulfilled before the day is over. The intention with this ploy is to encourage the dealing of traders on the floor. If they do not decide to deal by the time the day ends, they will not be earning their commission, making it a great incentive for them to put these trades high on their priority lists. When it comes to certain brokers, orders that are stop limit can only be used on a daily basis, meaning that they would have to be re-placed the next day if they were not filled in time.

Being aware of these options trading terms will help you come up with the perfect strategy to suit your financial situation as well as personality and knowledge levels. As I mentioned earlier, this is not about finding the perfect strategy that works for everyone, but about crafting your own unique method that works for you. The building blocks provided in this chapter will be a fantastic start for any beginner trader.

Chapter 5: The Importance of an Exit Strategy

At least equally important as, or even more important than deciding when to enter a trade is knowing exactly when you will exit. This is something that many traders, especially beginners, struggle with first determining and then sticking with. For this reason, trading is as much about will power as it is about anything else. Too many traders that are extremely and knowledgeable fall victim to getting ahead of themselves and not getting out in time, meaning that they earn big and cannot resist the temptation of winning bigger, and end up losing it all. Be smart, and get in the habit of using pre-determined stops every time you trade.

You MUST have a Stop Decided Ahead of Time, Every Time:

It is of the utmost importance that you know exactly when you will leave a trading position, whether this be a position that ends up being highly profitable or not. A lot of people do not enjoy placing stops at all, with themselves or brokers. While this is understandable, you have to at least have an exit in mind, and as soon as you reach the appropriate tie, you have to act on the idea if that stop becomes breached. You should also always keep in mind the time that you will wish to take on profits and act on this as well when and if the scenario comes up.

Write it Down and Stick with it:

You can decide upon a stop mentally, making it so that the makers of the market can't follow exactly what you're trying to do and shift the price artificially to attempt to manipulate you. Once you decide on a stop mentally, make sure you record it on paper and stick with it no matter how hard it may be. Where you decide to place these stops is obviously your choice, but typically, when it comes to stocks, you should place them in a position that is above the appropriate resistance or support area. For example, some expert traders only choose to trade breakouts near resistance and support, making their stops positioned logically every time.

Look at Stock Prices instead of Option Prices when Determining Stops:

You may be tempted to keep a close eye on the prices of options, but it is actually smarter to look at the prices of stocks instead when you are coming up with a point for stops. This applies unless you are in a situation where you are trading with multiple legs or are trading spreads, or when you using intraday to trade options (not recommended for beginners).

Keep Emotions in Check when the Time Comes:

When you come upon the situation where you must make the exit you decided upon before entering the trade, it is likely that you will experience a whole range of emotions, from reluctance, to defiance, to impulse. What truly separates the mediocre traders from the greats who will go on to earn big is the ability to stick with their principles regardless of the emotion of the moment. This is something that may be difficult at first, but that can be improved upon as you grow as a trader.

Chapter 6: Fundamental Analysis Information

Fundamental analysis is a technique that uses the study of businesses on an individual level, paying attention to a few key aspects of the company and how it performs. This is the way that many professional investors find the information that will lead them to making the best and wisest investments with the greatest payoffs. This is something that any newbie to the options trading world should learn about and master. Among the aspects that fundamental analysis pays attention to are:

- **Profit of the Company.**
- **Revenue.**
- **Borrowings.**
- **The Company's Assets.**

To put it in a simple and easily understandable way, many of the important ratios of finance that you can find are combinations or manipulated versions of the four main items listed above. For this reason, getting familiar with each of them is a wise approach to constructing personalized strategies for options trading.

Why is Learning about Fundamental Analysis Important?

This is such an important aspect of trading because the share price of a company is, in essence, the reflection from the market of the value of that company. If there is a business that earns profit and that profit is growing each year, while the business manages to keep borrowings to low amounts and revenue continuously increasing, you have found a great business to place your investment in, as long as you can reasonably expect the trends of the company to continue.

Keep in mind that the prices of stocks are driven primarily by the expectations of people and that expectations are driven by whatever the sentiment is at the current time. Sentiment is mostly influenced by history of the past and news stories. News, when it comes to the level of corporations has to do with the financial results of a company and the future plans of that company. Considering this from a larger perspective, the economy, both internationally and nationally influences news.

How do Fundamental Considerations Affect the Prices of Stocks?

When looking at a company from the lens of fundamental analysis, there are some key considerations to take into account. Those are:

- **The Company's Management and History:** How does this company function and what does it do? How well has this business done in past sales and overall? How does its management team measure up in comparison to other companies? Does this business exist within a sector or industry that seems to have a future of prosperity where the services and goods provided will be needed in the future? When looking at the management of the company, are there signs of consistently rising revenue and earnings? All of this is extremely relevant information and many people who invest decide where to invest based on this information alone.

- **Results and News about the Price of the Stock:** For this definition, news refers to the economy as a whole, the world in general, the specific sector the stock is in, as well as the business itself. For example, in this case news could mean prices of a certain good (like oil) rising intensely and what effects this may have on the market. This could involve higher costs for transportation which could lead to prices of production going up, more inflation, and then higher rates of interest. All of that would have a negative impact on a lot of companies as they see rises in their base costs, which would affect their profitability all around and their margins.

The idea that inflation could occur at any time and the way some businesses utilize higher rates of interest to fight against this is an issue that many stocks have attached to them, in general. When the overall sentiment is tense and anxious about the possibility of high rates of inflation, markets may suddenly turn more volatile and uncertain, eventually falling. It is perfectly possible, and not uncommon, that news on stocks have pervaded the market and affected the movements of stocks in a negative way.

Results reflecting the earnings of a company show the performance financially of an individual business and in America get published every quarter of a year (and every half year in the UK). It's important to note here that the most crucial numbers you can pay attention to are the numbers that show the earnings both generally and on a per share basis of the company.

- **The Expectations and Sentiments of People:** It's commonly spoken around investing circles that emotions of people have a lot to do with the movements of the market, but is this fair to say? Well, fear and greed certainly have a large impact on the way prices fluctuate in the context of nearly any market out there. How is it possible that a business that has no history and barely any earnings can get valued as high as a billion? Is it because the business has certain technology that can shift the globe as a whole? Perhaps the business has very convincing techniques for marketing and a strategy for growth that investors are drawn to, deciding the value of the company from what they expect it to earn.

The sentiment of the market does not always work in a way that is logical, and at times, it's hard to understand why some companies seem to do well while others don't. This sentiment controls the expectations of how the business will perform in the future, and as humans, we know that sentiment can change quickly in everyday life. The expectations of humans come in many different forms, when it comes to the results of a company and also in regards to the recommendations of analysis of the share price of the business.

It is actually quite incredible how far off the recommendations can be of analysts. Obviously, there is no person in the world that can always be right, but at times, the analysts are not even close to being correct. For this reason, you should always be careful accepting the recommendations of analysts. Most people who work as analysts, in the past, have been employed by firms that wished to perform business with businesses that they were doing the reports on. That would explain why it was rare to see "sell" recommendations on stocks, even in the case of sells that appeared obvious.

- **The Economy as a Whole:** Before you delve into the fundamentals of a specific company, you should take the time to look at the basics of economics first. Many people are intimidated or put off by the subject of economics, but here, there's no need for that. In the grand scheme of investing, we are only discussing the most common of common sense, and the best place to begin is with the overall climate economically of the country as a whole. The official name for this approach is looking at things from the "top down". What this means is that you are viewing things from a perspective of the big picture. To say it another way, how well is the economy performing, in general? Do you see any potential issues on the horizon?

This approach makes a lot of sense, since the success you will have or not have depends entirely on paying attention to what is happening all around you in the market. Although this may sound daunting, it really doesn't require too much effort. You only need to stay aware of what is going on in the news, which will allow you to have enough knowledge to have a feel for what is happening in economics.

After this, you can begin chaining occurrences into scenarios that are likely to happen in the future. Keep in mind that this is not a book about economics, but some key figures exist that have an extreme amount of importance in whichever economy you live in on the planet. There are some key numbers you can keep an eye on to get an idea of the overall economy of any given country at nearly any time:

- **Reports on Employment:** Consisting of two distinct surveys, the establishment survey and the household survey, employment reports show the figures of the rate of unemployment. This will give you an extra glimpse into the economic status of a country as a whole.

- **The Sales in Retail of the Region:** This figure is the result of the receipts resulting from stores on a retail level around the area. These are often measured without taking into consideration gasoline, food, and automobile figures, since it's the monthly changes that you should look at to determine how demands are shifting on a consumer level. Sales figures on a retail level do not count services that have to do with spending, which accounts for more than half of consumption as a whole in modern day.

When it comes to economics, nearly everything essentially comes down to the amount of supply versus demand. What items are priced at is the direct result of this. A lot of indicators on an economic level exist to give us guidance so we can construct our own assessments of what this looks like in the economy as a whole. When you observe indicators economically of any kind, you should follow along with the trail that considers what supply and demand effects will take place.

- **Building Permits and Housing Startups:** Starts are defined as the start of the excavating of foundations for buildings and mostly have to do with residential building. These starts are a measure of the amount of housing units that have started being constructed every month. These are led by something known as permits for building, which are a prerequisite for the excavations. However, these permits are not necessary everywhere, so looking at the starts figures can be more informational. These figures are known for being volatile, since they are affected wildly by natural disasters and extreme seasonal weather.

You could look, for example, at the rates of unemployment. If it goes up, what affect will this cause in the overall economy of the place? With less people working and businesses making cuts on their employment, it's safe to assume that citizens in that area will not have as much to spend there. People who are still employed may not have as much job security, meaning that they might wish to save more money and spend less.

This can lead to the demand for certain services and goods decreasing (like leisure items or furniture), resulting in lower profits and revenue for companies that center around leisure, retail, and goods. As an investor, it's your job to consider what type of effect this will have in the stocks involved in sectors like that.

Paying Attention to Basic Principles in the World of Supply and Demand:

Prices will go up when demand gets higher than the available supply. This will happen because the demand either gets out of control or the supply gets bottlenecked or restricted in some other way. For example, if a negative harvest in oranges happens, the prices for oranges will go up inevitably, whether the demand stays the same or not, since the overall equilibrium has changed in some way.

Sometimes, demand will go down in relation to the available supply, leading to the drop of prices. It's rare that sales in the winter at stores will have clothing that is highly popular. Typically, you will see products that are classified as inventory that needs to be cleared, in order to make room for trendier and newer items. This is the well-known case of declining demand for outdated items so businesses can get rid of items in a cheap and effective way, which explains why shoppers get the best deals when sales are coming to an end. These bargains, unfortunately, will be the garments that are the least attractive. You will also find that these sale items come in less popular sizes, since they are all that is left over.

What can be Learned from these Trends in Supply and Demand?

This is just one example of the proof of the way supply and demand affect each other. When there is a steady relationship between supply and demand, this will lead to overall steady figures in prices and values of services and products. The relationship between the two is inescapable, and every smart trader knows how to pay attention to these trends to their own benefit. Start seeing these patterns in your everyday life and this will translate to becoming a better investor.

How to Navigate the Marketplace Rules of Trading:

A lot of myths exist out there that have been accepted and passed along by everyone, although they are very easy to disprove. One of these popular myths is about the market of real estate performing at a higher capacity in times of higher inflation or can be used as a quality hedge to combat the effects of inflation. This myth is highly untrue, and a closer look at the facts of the situation will prove it. However, too many people accept it as truth without a second thought.

Don't try to be a Fortuneteller, instead, Trade on Reliable Facts:

It is too common for new traders to fall into the trap of trying to forecast and predict every little motion of their stock. A lot of people fall prey to their own whims of seeing what they wish to see, rather than viewing what is happening in reality. You need to stay aware of exactly what is happening, staying conscious of indications that show that the reality may shift, but don't fall into trying to predict the future. Warren Buffett has been quoted as claiming that forecasting will tell you more about the person trying to forecast than it will about the future. Keep in mind that attempting to predict the future with stocks is more like gambling than trading, and that is not what you're here to do.

How to Use Knowledge about Human Nature to your Advantage with Investing:

Keep in mind that not much changes when it comes to the market. People will always stay people. Greed, fear, and hype are overarching qualities in humans as a whole. The stock market is always affected by situations in the economy on a wide scale, including the ones listed in this chapter and other situations, like announcements from governments or the prices of oil. Both of these can lead to people buying in the short term due to panic, or selling for the same reason, or some combination of the two.

Stay in the know about these items of news and how they will impact the swings of volatility in the short term of the market. In general, markets have huge disorders of the personality, and as investors, we must learn how to interpret this information and stay with our guiding principles, no matter what those are. Looking at the market in this way can be helpful for understanding the unpredictable motions that can occur within it. Keeping this in mind will help you stay impervious to motions that can be devastating to unsuspecting investors.

A Valuable Metaphor about the Market from a Professional Investor:

A legendary and inspirational investor named Benjamin Graham once wrote a book in which he referred to the market as a manic depressive who is prone to extreme mood swings and changing his mind erratically about values in mere moments. This can be a valuable way of viewing the market, leading us to the fact that the value of a stock on an intrinsic level is not changing, meaning that your opinion should not shift when you invest for long term goals. People who invest in the short term usually do not care about a share's values intrinsically and typically will focus a lot more on indicators of technical analysis. When it comes to this type of trading, having an outlook like that is suitable, but when it comes down to it, only you can choose what type of trading works best for your lifestyle.

Chapter 7: The "Common Sense" Strategy to Trading Options

The foundation of any effective trading strategy is having common sense and staying aware of what is going on around you. It seems almost too simple and easy to be true, but this basic philosophy goes a long way.

What are Some Examples of Common Sense that could Pay Off in Investing?

- Noticing that specific trucks of retail stores are all over the road, pointing to the fact that people all over the place are ordering items from the business.

- New products suddenly showing up in everyone's house. For example, large clocks with a digital display along with thermometers and temperature displays. It is a smart idea to find out who creates these clocks by looking at the product's backside. You can then figure out whether the business exists in the stock market or is already the subsidiary of a business that exists in the stock market.

- Paying attention to mature businesses. Most investors look around for stocks that pay high dividends, but focusing on companies that have existed for a long time and have reliable cash cow portions of their business is a good idea. You should also look for companies that don't need much reinvestment to continue experiencing high sales numbers.

- Which toys appear to be trendy at the moment with your friends' children or your own? Which company has the rights to distribution and marketing for these items?

The approach to options trading that relies on common sense has been supported and endorsed by famous investors like Peter Lynch and even Warren Buffett. In our modern day, there is less of an excuse than ever to be behind on the latest information about stocks and options. The world wide web has made it so that everyone can find the information they need on any given subject, including trading and investing in options. Conducting research on nearly any subject is easier than it has ever been. Simply search for the item you need to find out about and quickly and reliably, you will have an ocean of information at your fingertips within a few short moments.

Some Key, Common Sense Factors to Remember in Investing Options:

Any way you look at it, common sense is a necessary factor in trading and choosing which stocks you will follow. If it turns out that you have found an indicator that seems reliable and is telling you that there is a downward trend on the market, is it a good idea to start purchasing stocks? While some may say that quality stocks are quality stocks no matter what, and while this is true in a sense, it isn't very wise to purchase stock in a company that is heading downward. Keep in mind that, in investing, it doesn't pay to try to be too smart.

We dedicated a large portion of the first chapter of this book to patience in investing, and it's so important that it deserves to be revisited. Be patient with waiting for a sector to start moving downward, and then jump in. Keep in mind that trying to forecast or predict movements isn't a good idea. Investing is not fortunetelling. However, you ideally want to know how to figure out the direction a stock is moving when it appears to be shifting.

Look for Tools that Reveal Overall Direction in the Market:

A lot of products for software even have personalized indicators that can show an overall direction of the market in a reasonably reliable fashion. Common statistics will reveal that over half of the percentage of the movement of a stock can be attributed to the overall direction of the market, while about a third of the percentage of its motion can be attributed to the direction of its sector. Perhaps it isn't so surprising, then, that you will enjoy greater success and improve your chances as a whole if you look for a reliable tool for figuring out the direction of the market overall.

With the Common Sense Strategy, Timing is a Key Component:

It's completely impossible for everyone in the world to be correct, and this includes the doomsday prophets who are constantly claiming that the end of times is near. But, timing definitely has a huge role to play in determining how profitable a market will be. Successful investors from all walks of life are aware of the fact that one method for improving overall timing is utilizing tools or indicators that show which direction markets are heading in a prevailing way. Another way to improve timing is utilizing the analysis method known as technical analysis, or the technique that relies on price chart interpretation.

Common Sense means Exercising Caution with Accepting Advice:

A smart line of advice to follow is that every investor should take the recommendations of gurus with a huge grain of salt. Financial specialists can, at any given moment in time, be receiving pressure to hand out certain recommendations and tailored lists to people listening, which makes their advice iffy at best, unreliable at worst. If you do receive advice from an expert, be sure to pay attention to what they have to gain from the advice.

You should also be careful about receiving advice from well-intentioned friends. If someone has more experience than you in any given area of life, it can be tempting to take their words of advice to heart, but investing is a highly personal journey. For this reason, you should only listen to your own knowledge and experience and do your best to learn from your mistakes when building your options trading strategy.

Conclusion

Thank you again for buying this book!

I hope this book was able to help you to feel more knowledgeable about the world of trading options. The goal with this book was to show you that this activity is suitable for anyone who is ready to commit to it. There is definitely a learning curve with this subject, but with the right attitude and a commitment to persistence and learning, you can achieve your trading goals.

The next step is to use the knowledge you have gained to begin doing practice trades, start taking notes on your successes and losses, and get better and better with time. When starting out, everyone suffers losses with options trading. That's just how it goes, and there's no way to prevent it. However, you can learn to view these "setbacks" as valuable learning experiences that make you a better trader in the long run. If you adopt this mindset, you will be well on your way to dominating options trading.

Finally, if you enjoyed this book, then I'd like to ask you for a favor, would you be kind enough to leave a review for this book on Amazon? It'd be greatly appreciated!

Head Over To Amazon Now To Leave a Review!

www.ingramcontent.com/pod-product-compliance
Lightning Source LLC
Chambersburg PA
CBHW071828200526
45169CB00018B/1254